MW01424018

My Teacher

Autumn Leigh

REAL LIFE readers™

Rosen Classroom™

New York

My teacher reads.

My teacher writes.

My teacher draws.

My teacher paints.

My teacher plays too!

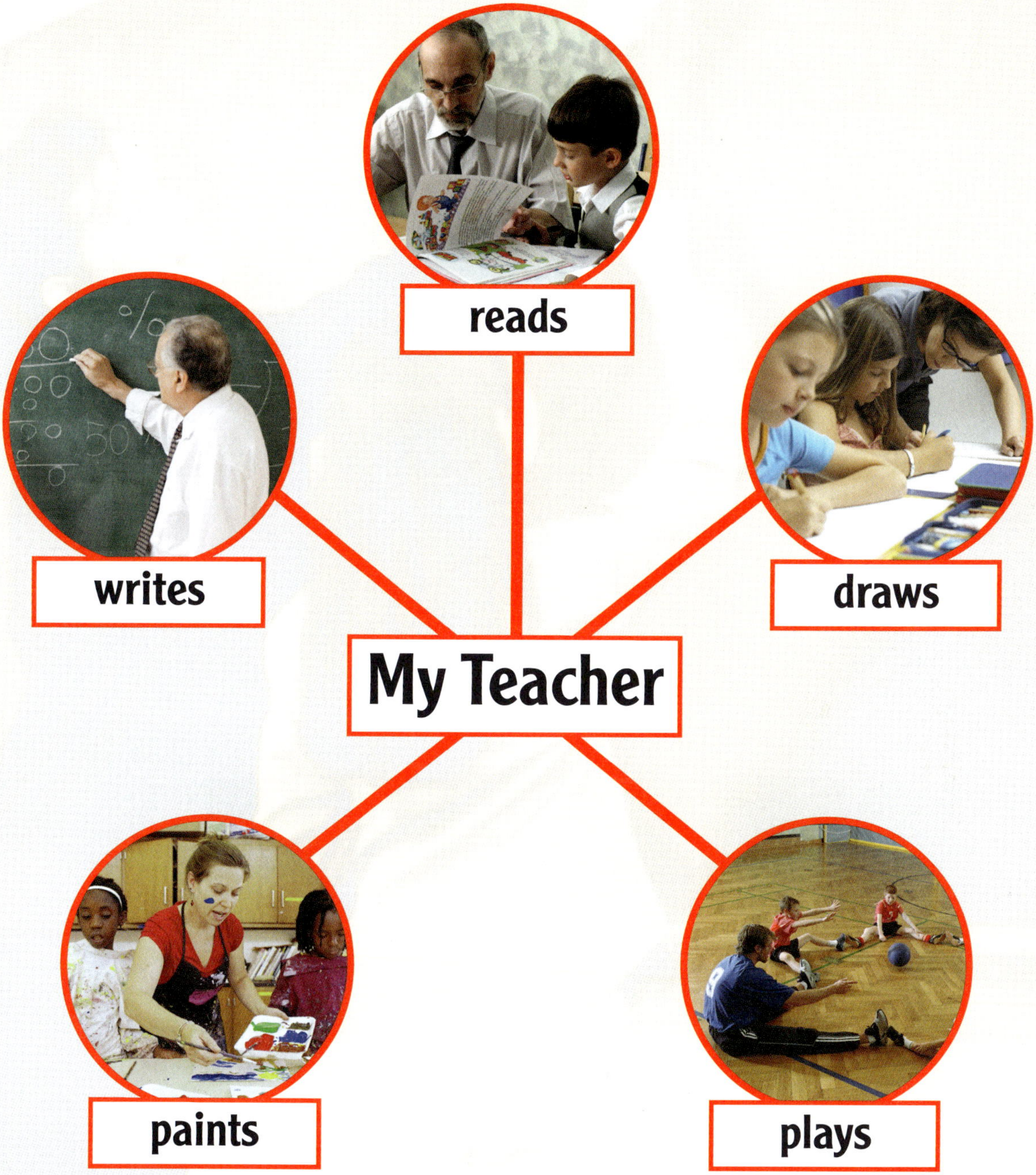
reads
writes
draws
My Teacher
paints
plays

Words to Know

draw

paint

play

read

write